CRY BABY

Nivine Jay

THANK YOU

HEY GUYS I WROTE A FUCKING POETRY BOOK! Can I say fucking in this?? (Sorry mom).

I had my first real heart break Easter of 2016. Jesus rose and my boyfriend kicked me out.. I thought I had everything figured out and BAM just like that it felt like it was all ripped away in a moment. Poetry helped me find a way to process my feelings without turning everything into a big joke. Here are the layers of my healing process all laid out for you to read, relate to, laugh at, cry along with.

To everyone that gave me a shoulder to cry on, a couch to sleep on, a meal to eat, an Adderall to think, a Xanax to sleep, THANK YOU. You kept me going. For all the nice girls in club bathrooms that cleaned the puke off of my hair, THANK YOU. To my cousin Dina who answered every single one of my phone calls (even when she was in the shower)and always had a meme to make me laugh THANK YOU. For every bad Tinder date, I went on to forget about my broken heart, THANK YOU (for feeding me). To the CVS employees that let me sit on the floor and cry in the vitamin section, you are the real heroes here.

If any of you are going through a break up right now please know that it will pass. I promise. Those feelings go away. Then they will come back (no one tells you that part) but they will go away again. Love yourself the way you want them to love you.

And last but not least, to any boy that has ever made me cry, **FUCK YOU.**

SPECIAL NOTE FROM MY SISTER:

Hey everyone, this is Nour, Nivine's sister. She's allowing me to be a part of this because I told her I would curse her life if she didn't mention me in a book one day. So, listen up people. Here's some advice I can give. Marry rich and don't complain. Just kidding, see, I'm funny too. Let me tell you something about my sister. When we were young, she always followed me around and did ridiculous things for my attention, such as opening candy wrappers for me in target, and asking my mom permission for me to shave my legs because I was chicken shit. Now here I am, realizing she's the one that I try to become, she's my little sister, and yet here I am, wanting to be more and more like her. If you enjoy this book, it's just the beginning. Nivine is going to rule the world.

CONTENTS

CHAPTER 1
DENIAL

a defense mechanism in which confrontation with a personal problem or with reality is avoided by denying the existence of the problem or reality.

OUT OF THIS WORLD

PART 1
There was a time
When I thought you a star and I a rocky planet
When I believed it was just me
Unwillingly orbiting your being
But now I know that you are a black hole
Countless planets pulled into your gravity
Knowing their fate
is to die within your radiance

PART 2:
I can no longer tell
If I am still in an orbit
around you
If I am just longing
for you
out of habit
Or if I have been lucky enough
To escape your gravity
Entirely.

PART 3
To me you were an entire galaxy.
You were a galaxy and I was just a rock
A hopeless minuscule piece of meteorite
That you'd seen a million times.
You were this perfect and wonderful galaxy
That I'd seen a million times
But each time I looked at you
I found a new constellation
Once you've seen a meteorite, you've seen them all.
But there's only one galaxy.

HOME

You asked me when I wanted to go home
I wanted to tell you that for me home has never been a
place
I wanted to tell you that while I don't live here
I am already home
Home is where you are
instead I just say
"Whenever, whatever is best for you"
I cannot begin to describe my elation when you said
"Stay as long as you like"
At last,
I am home.

REAL LOVE

We tethered our fingers into knots
So we could not forget what we had
& what we had not
The wind pushed us towards the shore
Held up by the numbers
Held up by the time
Real love leaves you somewhere
other than where you started

IF I COULD

— if I could I would
give you my all
Maybe I could
I don't want to
You've never known
my worth
I am not ready
To be your backup
even though I want to
even though I would love to
so, this is me
not apologizing for
not letting you
devour the pieces
of my soul and heart
so, this is me
letting you know
that even
if I could
I surely wouldn't
So, this is me
because you never really got to see that side
All you saw was someone stupid enough
To believe all your white lies.

CO-DEPENDENCY

All I am is a glass bottle
That contains no message
floating in undiscovered oceans
Finally, one-day I stumble upon land
Graced by the rough hugs of the sands
And the incomparable warmth of your hands
And there I sat still as you filled me
But then it only made me feel emptier
I couldn't adapt my volume
To your turbulent weather
My cork held everything in
And my bottle neck
Suffocated me
So, the cracks appeared
And I started to drip
Without ever letting myself fully break

BAD HABIT

I'm beginning to realize
I have a bad habit of hurting
the ones who love me most,
and loving the ones
who hurt me the most.

Mountains

why do I move mountains
for people who
won't even walk down the street
to see me

Consumer

Let's fill this place with stuff
that makes us think
that makes us feel
like with this stuff
there's things to feel
a better feel
something more real
ring on ring on ring
in rusted flakes
and faker things
and everything you ever bought
would either fade
or break or bring
out everything but happy feels
and constant pleasure
we call it trash
we called it treasure

<u>HARD</u>

You were easy to love and hard to leave
Sadly, I was hard to love and easy to leave

WANT

First, they want you

Then they want more of you

Then they want everything about you

Then they want less of you

Until they want nothing of you

Here we go again:
jealousy
Hunger
Stemming out of fear.
Keep me near, let me hear
that, even when you're surrounded by thousands, I'm
the only one
your heart is beating for.

TRUTH OR DARE

You do not get to choose who you love
That is the sad truth
For I could be head over heels for you
I just can't find the words to get through
I gawk at you while you gaze at another
I lie and say I see you like a brother

UNHEALTHY

Our love time travels into other worlds and dimensions.

In each one you save me
time after time.

You saw me in the dark almost a shadow myself.
Bleeding into the background, denying myself the light.

So, you came to me.
Fire in your hands.

You ignited my soul once more.

The darkness is now my shadow for I am burning light
again.

Falling in love with you over and over again

Fragment of fire
lasting till the end

in every lifetime

my heart burns for you.

TEARdrops

We are just simple teardrops
waiting for our fall
down the cheek
to the floor
where we can evaporate
or just be swept away and become
no more
We are everything wrapped
in a tight little bow.
So perfect, yet so chaotic.
Beauty born, created, destroyed,
ready to unfold

CHAPTER 2
ANGER

*a strong feeling of annoyance,
displeasure, or hostility*

HOLDING:

Everyone talks about how hard it is to let go.
We never talk about how insanely difficult holding on is.
When the other person doesn't care if you let go.
It takes all of you.
all of you mentally
all of you physically
everything you have got.
I was always tired from staying up all night thinking
about you and over analyzing our entire relationship.

Picking my brain trying to pin point what I did to fuck
up. The worst part is when I started to become the
entertainment for your boredom.
You'd play with me like an old toy, soon realizing why
you put it down so long ago in the first place.
You wore me out and tore me apart
piece by piece
just to put me back down again as if I was

untouched.

REMEMBER WHEN I MISSED YOU

I envisioned what kind of father you'd be
I failed to see
All the hurt that you'd later inflict upon me
Remember when I missed you?
I mistook heaven for yet another tool
Oh what a fool love can be
Just another lover lost at sea
Remember when I missed you?
Now all I can do is resist the thought that you exist
You'd ignore my texts
and you still ask for a kiss
All of a sudden you've become unmissed
Oh what a twist
Remember when I missed you?

NO VACANCY

The way you looked at me it felt like summer.
You listened and laughed
I felt relevant
suddenly my voice mattered
I was no longer empty
I was your summer time.
You and I. Always.

The seasons do change
winter came
your cold breeze
Left me frozen.
The sunlight hitting our faces was dimmed
my memories soaked in over saturated filters
where did our love go?
I asked myself as I soaked my bed in tears
Every night I cried for you.
Where is our love?

It was within me all along
You were winter and I was summer
The light was in me
No more endless nights of you
Occupying my time.
There is only occupancy for one person
me.
It will always be me

There are no other vacancies.

I AM ALL MY EDGES

I am the quick wit that flies out of my mouth
at inappropriate times
I am the gasps of fresh air in-between abundant
laughter
I am that dull ache when your heart is about to break

I am the words "almost" and "maybe"
I am the square piece that tried to fit in the hole
to fit for you. No matter how cold
Tried to contort to your circle
The same girl that tried to soften her edges
Just so we could fit
Just to show you that
maybe just maybe
I could be worth it

I am a fraud
I have dulled my edges
I am not meant for this hole
Maybe I'm meant for nothing at all
I am the square piece that tried so hard to fit
So now I sit here
Feeling worthless
Waiting for love

You find a round peg
You ask me to move over
I came all this way
and all I got from you was a cold shoulder

ONE NIGHT

The brighter their smile
The darker their deeds
I have one rule.
I live by it every time.
It was meant to protect me from mistakes like you.
Share a bed and never speak again.
A night with a stranger to fill the void.
I have one rule.
A cure for a night.
I broke it.
I let you in.
You built me up just to break me down.
I broke my own rule letting you in

just to break me.

CHAPTER 3
Bargaining

*The **bargaining** stage may occur prior to loss as well as after loss, as an attempt to negotiate pain away*

pretty
I write pretty words
for you
and I paint the prettiest pictures
of us
in my mind
as if I think they will
bring you to
me.

WHISPERS

I whispered, "I love you"
It was quiet and softly hidden under my breath
I knew you wouldn't hear me utter those words.
I said it as my arms wrapped around your shoulders,
and I held you so I could fall asleep.
I whispered those words behind your back, on your
right side
hoping that they would softly caress your skin and find
a way into your heart so that maybe, even though they
were whispered.
You would feel the warmth and truth behind them and
one day want to whisper those same words back to me.

Do you love me?

I could see our future in your eyes
I begged you to see
you ask me to get down on my knees
I allow you to use me endlessly

DON'T GO

PART 1
Don't go.
I will give you a million reasons why.
I'll even believe all your little white lies Don't let me
down
I will change, I beg and plead
Have you forgotten how much this means to me Don't
go.
I kick and scream
tell me it was just all just a dream

PART 2
I've been so forgiving
this I know
countless times you've let me down
when I needed you the most.
yet still, I miss you.
I forgive you time and time again
because I miss you.
It's better to forgive you
Than to watch you go.

Run away with me

You don't have to say yes
But don't say no.
You'll change your mind
When you imagine the places, we'll go
Run away with me
We'll take your BMW
And venture down the open roads
Let the stars guide us
Leave our anger back home
Run away with me
We'll stay in pretty motels
Or we can drive all night
Let's dance in bars
Stay up talking until daylight
So, run away with me

Before I said you didn't have to say yes
but say yes. We can be happy.
You don't have to run away with me

But please
don't go.

CHAPTER 4
DEPRESSION

Depression is a constant feeling of sadness which is believed to stem from a chemical imbalance in the brain

BROKEN

You made me feel like you would
give me all the stars in the sky
in the end you couldn't even give me a proper
goodbye.

WHO'S TO BLAME

To feel shame
To see shame
To be shame.
You're the only one I
Blame. Will I ever be the same?

OBSOLETE

Words just disappear
Silence fills my ears
Flooding my head
I miss you in my bed
Your side now tear soaked
You haunt my sleep
I become obsolete
Wondering if anyone's side
Of the street is ever really neat

Strangers are offering me treats.

ALRIGHT

So much of my head is fucked right now.
I'm content and happy and chilled.
I'm stressed out, anxious and unfulfilled.
I thought by now I'd feel something like peace.
But all around me is apathy.
I was strong and sure of who I was.
Now I've sobered in the night.
I had goals and dreams and plans for life.
Now it's a struggle to say I'm alright.

Inconsistency

I can see this world
through a different lens
perspective focused
perspective distant
this shit
that shit
inconsistent

CAN'T BE TAMED

My mother didn't teach me to be brave
She never let me cross the streets
Without her sending a wave
So, tell me why I crave
danger like a moth to a flame
What is this sick game.
I have a deep sense of shame
When I watch you look up and down my frame
I am not someone you can tame
I was never taught to be brave
So forever I will be a slave
Sitting and staring out of the window
From afar I will watch them wave as I tremble
When you put your fingers on my temples
You slowly move them down to the curve of my back
Why do all guys have to be like that?

I CRUMBLE

I silently speak to the night
Harmonize my heartbeat
by crushing the covers
in to my chest
But it was cold
The night whispered back
It fills my head with
doubts and despair
Froze the streams of tears
to my face
Broke my heart rate
into fragments
I lay motionless
But inside
a world was working
And it was crumbling
like a cliff side
All because you
whisper the words,
"We need to talk"

Game Over

The laughter is gone
The excitement is gone
The joy is gone
All replaced by one thing...
Nothing.
Lost in your mind
Trapped in an endless loop
This is now life
Life is scary
Life is meaningless
Life is over.

HURRICANE

I always envied storms.
I wished to be as strong as they were.
I shared this with you
You giggled and told me I was nothing more
than a gust of wind
That is exactly what you said to me that night
You were always so fight or flight
You scream and try to break down my walls
Don't you know I'm not meant to fall?
I will sit still and I will smile
But before I speak will you sit next to me
This looks like it's going to take a while.
You kneel right here so sweet
You even have the audacity to reach for my cheek
As if I didn't just hear
all the negativity that you speak.
My love, don't ever forget.
About the storm that lies just beneath the surface
I am the winds and the whistles inside of them
"I am the storm.", I whimper and try to plead
"Honey, can you please get out of me"

Now you are on top and I can't break free
Why is it that no one ever sees me for me.
Why do you only see me as a body?

There was a void
in my heart so large
where your love
could've lived.
How was I able to
reserve such
a big space
for you
and leave so little
room to love
myself.

CHAPTER 5
ACCEPTANCE

Acceptance: This is the ultimate goal of the stages of *grief*! *Acceptance* doesn't mean that you like what is happening or what did happen. *Acceptance means* that you can acknowledge that something did or will happen. You have found some form of peace.

- An apology letter to myself.

"I forgive you
for pawning your mom's gold necklace
Those bambi eyes dripping tears
Those days we had not one single fear
survival on the mind
you didn't want to take the time
to stop and reflect
all you wanted was
to push down the feelings of neglect
I forgive you
For the strangers that you knew
weren't good enough but still
their fingertips found
their way onto your hips
you pretended that you liked it
I forgive you
for not screaming that you're worth it
That we are worth it.
I forgive you for your sharp tongue.
for all the times you said and did things that will never
be undone.
I forgive you for treating yourself like a
toxic waste sight when
you should've known all along you were
better than Turkish delights."

What If

My father always told me, "Show them what you're
worth"

I want to be reassured. I want to be brave enough to put
on a face and show them, but what is there to show?
What am I even worth, if anything at all?

"Don't let them underestimate you" he says to me
but what if they are right?

Its haunting and suffocating.

"What if" can be a beautiful thought
What if I am better and stronger than I think I am.

but nonetheless I still feel like pieces of broken glass
glued together sitting on the edge of a table
in the middle of an earthquake.

Keep Moving

The Tide Moves
always
in time
never
too fast
or slow
if only I knew
how to see life
that way

GIFTS

You broke my heart into
pieces
and shortly after
piece by piece
you collected me and
piece by piece
you're giving me myself back.

- *"I will help you recover what they took away from you, she said to me"*
- **Note to self.**

Trial and Error

How do you feel?
Is your heart aching?
Is it breaking?
Is it raking
Through the leaves
To find an empty spot,
A place where it can breathe?
Are you looking for an escape?
A gaping hole in the wall
Where you hope to push through
Fighting against it all
The hole is behind you,
There may be cracks,
A tear falls down,
You made it through
Trial and error,
But you made it through
Deep breath.
You made it.

ALL FOR YOU
The best thing you
Can do is let him go
watch him walk out the door.
As he moves further in the distance
Allow him to take all that pain
That clouded your eyes
So, you can seek the
Right path
That which was always
Meant for you.

ONE MOMENT

It takes **one single moment**
One little thought
One action
One movement can change the entire world
Do not make yourself smaller for
It could be you that changes it all

LETTER TO MY YOUNGER SELF:

people will call you a mess.
a messy hurricane of opinions
and passions and laughter and tears,
people will try and tell you this is a flaw.
this is your biggest strength.
Don't ever stop being a mess of a woman.
be wild and fiery and hard to swallow.
continue to storm out of rooms.
slam your fists on tables.
never stop raising your voice when
they try to shut you up
let it echo like thunder.
they will tell you to be gentler.
to be calm like a stream.
do not listen please
why would you want to be gentle like a stream
when you are already an ocean.
the strongest ocean moves even the sturdiest
of rocks. let yourself overflow with
emotions. whether they are good or bad
let them exit you like a volcanic eruption
you will find yourself spinning from corner
to corner. like an eager tornado. do not let anyone
convince you to sit ideally by.
you were born to disrupt the peace
make a dent
go ahead and demolish the old
like an angry forest fire.
while they all tell you you're too much.
only you know that its only once
you've burned it all down
can you begin to regrow.

Look I'm not a bad guy.
I see myself as a guy with a heart of gold
and the best of intentions.
But sometimes things just don't work out
and the reasons behind a break-up are complicated.
Even when there is real love between two people.
So, I like to look at the bright side of things, like this book.
Wow! It's a special work. It's raw, it's real; it's a revelation.
It's an honest look inside the heart
and soul of a real live human being.
And I am proud to be a part of it.
The other bright side is our stories.
They have a beginning, middle and an end.
but then they have new beginnings, new middles and new ends.
It's a constant cycle.
If you look at a life from 10,000 feet away,
it's a wavy line, gently rising and falling.
We have our highs and our lows, on and on.
Where life leads, we don't know,
but the trajectory is always up.
Like this book.
Another high.

ABOUT THE AUTHOR

Nivine Jay is a Lebanese nutcase living in Los Angeles writing about herself in third person while consuming Dominos pizza. Her accomplishments include crying at fancy restaurants, pronouncing words wrong, being in a constant state of confusion, and perfecting the deer in the headlights look.

CPSIA information can be obtained
at www.ICGtesting.com
Printed in the USA
LVHW021125070423
743752LV00001B/62

9 781388 806972